It's Time to #Slay

MY JOURNEY FROM NORMAL KID TO FRESH BORN UNICORN

nickelodeon

THAT GIRL Lay Lay

It's Time to #Slay

MY JOURNEY FROM NORMAL KID TO FRESH BORN UNICORN

by *That Girl Lay Lay*

with Kwyn Bader

SCHOLASTIC INC.

To my father for seeing my gifts early and pushing me to pursue them. To my mother for teaching me to never quit. And to all my fans— I love you! I do it all for you.

—That Girl Lay Lay

To kids who believe in their dreams.

—K. B.

CONTENTS

Chapter 1: Here to Slay...1

Chapter 2: Freestyle Famous 17

Chapter 3: What's Freestyle?.............................27

Chapter 4: Princess Slaya 35

Chapter 5: It Takes a Family 43

Chapter 6: Talking to the Universe 57

Chapter 7: Go Lay Lay Go! 65

Chapter 8: The Fresh Born Unicorn Meets Dapper Dan 79

Chapter 9: Work Hard, Play Harder 89

Chapter 10: Move Like I Move 99

Chapter 11: On Tour with Tha Slay Gang 107

Chapter 12: Gotta Eat Right 121

Chapter 13: Tha Lil Big Dripper! 127

Chapter 14: All the Way Lit 139

Chapter 15: That's a Rap 147

CHAPTER 1
Here to Slay

Hey, y'all! It's me, That Girl Lay Lay! Welcome to my book. You probably know me from TV, Instagram, YouTube, or even the radio as a rising hip-hop star who raps, dances, and acts. Maybe you've seen my *Ellen* performance or my music video "Supersize XL." Maybe you've watched my show on Nickelodeon or you've even been to one of my concerts. No matter what you've seen on-screen or onstage, it's only a part of me. I want y'all to get to know the *real* me better. So, this is my chance to be *your* girl Lay Lay!

From the time I could tie my own shoes, I've been all about one thing—music! I grew up on beats,

rhymes, and melodies. By the time I was five, I knew that I was going to pursue a life in entertainment. But I had no idea *how* I was actually going to make it! Now that I have, I can't wait to let you see inside the work and fun that went into developing my talent. And I want to share my stories about some of the people who helped me become the Lay Lay you hear on tracks and watch on TV!

SOME FACTS ABOUT ME:

🖤 My real name is Alaya High.

🖤 My hometown is Houston, Texas.

🖤 I'm a pescatarian, which means I eat fish but not red meat.

🖤 I was born on January 28, which makes me an Aquarius.

🖤 My favorite colors are pink and purple.

🖤 My favorite number is 28.

🖤 Although my performing name is That Girl Lay Lay, I've been known by other nicknames, too, including Fresh Born Unicorn, Princess Slaya, and Lil Big Dripper.

🖤 Two things about me that I'm most proud of are: I work hard AND I work hard to be a positive influence.

Hey Y'all

························ ························

I love hip-hop music.
Love it, love it, love it!
But there are so many
rap songs out there that
aren't right for kids.

·······························

Some have dirty lyrics or cuss words. Others tell rough stories we're not ready for. We start dancing to the beat, and then, without realizing it, we're repeating lyrics that are really negative and putting out bad messages that could get us in trouble. We need music that empowers us as girls and boys and still lets us flex our style and dopeness. I'm trying to show that you can rap positively from the heart and still slay. I'm letting people know, "You don't have to copy what they do. You can do something right for you."

In a million different ways, I'm just a regular kid. I like to watch TV and hang out with my friends. I do

some things right, but I also mess up a *lot*. I say the wrong thing, skip my house chores, and sometimes forget to do my homework.

In other ways, though, I'm not normal . . . at all. I mean, I have a *superpower*. I truly believe we all have one. Mine is performing in front of people. For some reason, that's what brings out the Wonder Woman in me. I can practice a dance move for days and mess it up every time, but then I'll step onstage . . . and I'll do it perfectly.

I'm Lay Lay, but when the camera comes on, I'm *Super* Lay Lay. I turn into this whole new person. I'm like, "Don't mess up. You got it. You got to be perfect."

Like the night in November 2018 when I performed during kids' night at a Houston Rockets

basketball game. Before the game started, I kept shooting basketballs because I knew I was going to be shooting a free throw on camera at halftime (after performing my song "Lit"). If I made the shot, $5,000 would be given to the Clutch City Foundation, which raises money for kids in need. So I really wanted to make it! But I missed every practice shot. EVERY single shot. As the saying goes, "I couldn't buy a basket."

Then, as soon as it was showtime and I walked to the free throw line in front of the camera, I could feel it. I was so far from the basketball hoop. But I had my *superpower*. I looked at the rim, took my shot, and made it! The camera made me feel like I was an NBA superstar—just like James Harden, whose jersey I was wearing that night!

During interviews after the game, I was telling everybody, "There was an angel on the rim because there's no way I made that. An angel pushed that ball in."

I'm very lucky to have a superpower when I need it, but that's not the only reason for my success; it's just one part of it.

I think, more importantly, I've worked really hard at my music and I've received love and support from people who want to see me succeed. And that started when I was just a little kid with a dream.

NBA superstar James Harden and me, outside the world famous Turkey Leg Hut in Houston, Texas.

"My dream was to go viral and get signed. Guess it came true!"

CHAPTER 2
Freestyle Famous

You could say I broke into hip-hop from the front seat of my dad's car. In the spring of 2018, when I was only eleven, my dad recorded my first-ever live freestyle on his phone. That one video changed my whole life. It made me famous. It seemed like it all happened overnight. But it really didn't. Because I basically grew up in a sound studio.

My dad, Acie High, is my biggest inspiration. He's been in the music game for a long time. He's a great rapper.

When I was little, I used to go to the studio with him a lot. I've always known I wanted to be some sort of entertainer, so I did everything I could to stay close to my dad and the music. I would come up with a million reasons why I didn't want to go to a babysitter or stay with my granny who ran her

Hanging with my dad, Acie High, between takes at
my video shoot with Young Dolph in Atlanta.

own day care center. My dad would get so tired of trying to make me go that he'd end up just taking me along to the studio instead—which was exactly what I wanted!

We would be there for hours while he recorded. I'd be on a phone, pretending I was playing a game or something, but really I was listening to him rap. My dad can write rhymes and also come up with something new and improvised right off the top of his head, which is known as freestyling. It was his freestyling that really inspired me and made me want to try it, too!

I can still remember my first rhyme when I was about five years old. We were at my house and there was some snack I wanted—probably Cheetos—and I caught my family off guard because I just started rapping!

It was like:

 We don't got no food in this house because we broke
We need to go to the store

No, it wasn't the greatest rhyme in the world. I mean, it didn't even *rhyme*! But it was my first freestyle!

As I got older, I started writing for myself and freestyling more and more. To spit good rhymes, you have to practice . . . and practice . . . and practice some more. You've got to find your flow—the smooth way rhythm and rhymes come together—and you've got to build your own vocabulary and discover your own style because hip-hop doesn't like copycats. So, I practiced my rhymes every day for years.

See what I mean? To the world, it looked like I became a rapper overnight, but I knew how much work I put into it!

And then, one day, I wrote this rap, and I was like, "Hey, Dad! I want you to record me doing this freestyle."

At first, he wasn't sure if he should record me. My dad really didn't want me in the rap world because he knew how hard it is to succeed without getting eaten alive by the business. The music industry is really tough and competitive. So many up-and-coming artists see their dreams go up in smoke when their music doesn't sell. And others have hit records but end up in debt to record companies because they signed bad contracts with people who took advantage of them.

But my dad could see I was totally dedicated. So right there in the car, he recorded me. I asked him to get his camera ready while I checked my edges and made sure my lip gloss was fresh. Then I just started rapping:

About to go live, yeah
Lay Lay 'bout to go live, yeah
Got scary vibes, yeah
Make all the kids go "Hi!" yeah

Then I became Super Lay Lay:

Turn me up when you play me
Little boys won't play me . . .

I was feeling it!

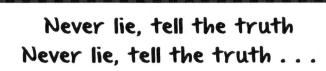

♪ **Never lie, tell the truth**
Never lie, tell the truth . . .

With every verse after that, I kept telling the truth *my* way. A week or two later, my dad finally posted the video on my Instagram page. And nothing was ever the same.

CHAPTER 3
What's Freestyle?

"GIRL BOSS"

FREESTYLIN'

efore I tell you more about the video, I should tell you a little bit about freestyle since it's a big part of hip-hop as a culture and what I do.

See, traditionally, freestyle rap has been rhymes that a rapper comes up with on the spot, either over a beat or a cappella. In other words, it's not written

Feeling free in my style at an interview for the *Hip Hop Weekly* YouTube channel.

out and memorized before performing. Freestyling has been part of the culture since the Stone Age of rap way back in the 1970s and '80s—when hip-hop was still being invented!

But I like to write out my raps, too. Writing gives me time to think things out more deeply. And then I still perform it with a "free style." I don't really like to put a label on what I do. I just want to do it with *freedom*.

If you've never spit a rap, give it a try! Write down a rhyme about your life or your friends, or try coming up with something right out of your imagination.

If you're just getting started, a small audience is all you need to give it a shot. See if your brother or sister, your parents, or a friend from school will listen to what you come up with. Or you can record your rap and listen back to yourself!

Freestyling is a super-fun way to express your creativity. I really encourage you to try it out, and don't give up! And you never know, if you keep trying, you might get good at it. Look at how far I've come since my hangry rap about Cheetos!

"We rap about all types of things. Food, pots and pans, butterflies . . . It don't even matter; we just rap."

CHAPTER 4
Princess Slaya

Fresh born unicorns hanging together.

N ow that I've given you the 411 on freestyle, let's get back to my story.

So, my "Shoot" video. (It's called that on the internet because that's the name of the track I was rapping over.) I didn't have any idea that it was going to go viral!

When my dad first posted it, I didn't totally get how Instagram worked. I had a handle, but I didn't really understand how to use it. At that point, I only had around 200 followers on the 'gram. And there are lots of cats and cars with more followers than that!

But in the next few days, my raps and videos started getting a lot of attention! I was like, "What am I getting all these likes for? What's going on?" Everything was going viral in a big way. The video I had filmed from the passenger seat of my dad's ride

was getting reposted on social media by people I never imagined would see it—including some of the best rappers in the business today. It got reposted by 50 Cent. Yep. *The* "Go, shorty, it's your birthday" 50 Cent! That made me feel amazing! Then I saw that T.I. posted about it. And Migos shouted me out!

And it wasn't just rappers. Mindy Kaling, one of my all-time favorite comedic actors and writers, had reposted it, too! One of my best friends called me and said, "Wow! You're famous! You're totally blowing up!"

It was crazy! Before I knew it, a bunch of record label execs were DMing me to see if I would want to sign with them: Atlantic, Empire, Def Jam—all the big labels! By the next week, they were flying me out to meet with them. In between meetings, my dad and I posted more videos made in his car, each getting more views than the last. By August 2018, only two and a half months from that first post, I signed with Empire Records, and I was officially part of the music world.

The "Shoot" video I made for my 200 followers

LAY LAY'S CELEB FANS

Quavo from Migos wanted to sign me to his label, but I'd already signed with Empire!

Getting inspiration from Colin Kaepernick at the 2019 Summer Jam Festival— where I also met Cardi B!

LAY LAY'S CELEB FANS

I was so happy to meet singer Tori Kelly in Atlanta. I'm one of her biggest fans!

Rapper Lil Baby hangs out at Turkey Leg Hut, too!

has now been viewed by over 400,000 people—and it's not even the most popular of my front-seat freestyles. And today I have more than one million followers on Instagram! That's a pretty big change!

So yeah, I became famous "overnight," but like I said, it also didn't happen "overnight." I had been working hard on my music for a long time.

I'm telling you because I want you to be successful, too. You just have to know that a LOT of hard work goes into getting what you want and becoming an "overnight" success. They may not realize it, but it's really the dedication, time, effort, and love that I put into my music that came through and impressed people. My viral video just made them take notice.

CHAPTER 5

It Takes a
Family

Princess Slaya

I was a very outgoing child.

I moved to Atlanta, Georgia, when I was eleven, but I'm *from* Houston, Texas. That's where I was born.

Houston was a great place to grow up, especially for me, because I had parents I really love and who

Born in Houston, raised by music!

love and want the best for me. Having them in my corner has helped me achieve my dreams.

My dad, Acie High, inspires me because I've seen him go through a lot in his own music career. I've watched him fall down and get back on his feet many times. He always stays motivated, especially when it comes to me doing well and staying safe in a tough industry. He never lets me see him down. And that's also what inspires me to do well.

After the "Shoot" video blew up and I got signed to Empire Records, I got to meet some of my rap idols—people whose work inspires me and influences my own music. I met Quavo from Migos, and Cardi B, too. But the coolest thing I realized is that, at the end of the day, no matter which big rappers I meet or listen to—I don't care if it's Kendrick Lamar, Jay-Z, or Chance the Rapper—my favorite rapper is, *and always will be*, my dad.

My dad is my role model and mentor when it comes to everything in life. He's been in this industry for longer than I've been alive, and he never lets anybody mess around with me when it comes to business deals. He studies all my contracts and works with lawyers to make sure everything is okay. He makes sure that I'm not "signing my life away." And I'm so grateful for that because a lot of kids in the entertainment industry don't have parents that look out for them properly. Some parents want the money and

Yeah, I'm a daddy's girl.

the fame more for themselves than for their kid.

But my dad is different. If I'm like, "Dad, hey, I'm not comfortable. I don't want to record this track," he's like, "Cool." He doesn't force me to do anything I don't want to do. Which is a good thing because, if you haven't figured it out yet, I'm very independent.

My dad's not *just* my dad. He's my best friend, too, and he always will be. I used to tell him when I was little, "When I become a teenager, I'm not going to be one of those kids who doesn't want their dad around."

And you know what? Now that I am a teenager, I still like hanging out with him. I'm like, "Hey, Dad, you want to go to the skating rink with me?"

So yeah, I'm a daddy's girl!

But guess what? I can be a momma's girl, too!

I love my mom, Antanique. Along with my dad, she's my biggest inspiration. My mom is amazing! She motivates me a lot. She's one of the strongest and most independent women I've ever known. Like my dad, she never lets anyone see her sad.

No matter what happens or what things get in the way, she keeps pushing through any challenges. In my eyes, Dad is Superman and Mom is Superwoman. I'm so lucky to have great parents who want me to achieve my goals. If they didn't have my back, there's no way I'd be successful!

But just so you don't think I get all my parents' attention, I also have an older sister, Sya, and three younger brothers, Cassius, Michell, and Ares (who's still a baby). We call Michell "Poppasay," and he's into music, just like me. He's all about

I'm a momma's girl, too!

a beat and some melody, and he knows every Michael Jackson dance, especially "Thriller." I can say, "Poppasay, perform this song!" and he's going to know it from start to finish.

Even though Cassius and Michell aren't *that* young, I still call them my babies. But they don't see themselves that way. I swear they think they're older than me. It's wild!

I like to hang out with them because they're so

funny. One time, I asked Cassius, "Cash, can I have a boyfriend?" He gave me a look and said, "Nope." As if he decided whether or not I'm allowed!

I said to him, "First of all, you're three. You don't even know what having a boyfriend means!"

So, I asked him, "Hey, do *you* have a little girlfriend?"

He says straight to my face, "Sure, I got a girlfriend."

Cassius thinks he's grown-up. He doesn't even know what a girlfriend is—I think he just likes the way it sounds.

And my brothers love to get into little fights with me. I guess that's pretty common with brothers and sisters. One time I got a bruise in the middle of my forehead from play boxing with Cassius. I didn't realize he could *really* fight! I mean, his name is *Cassius*—like Cassius Clay, better known as Muhammad Ali, who was pretty much the greatest boxer in history! But who knew my baby had it in him? He's really into books and school, so I didn't see him as trouble.

My dad was so mad when he found out! He said, "Look at what happened to your face! What are you going to do in your next interview?"

I looked in the mirror and was like, "What's the big deal? It's just a little bruise."

Honestly, I thought it was going to go away in a few days, but it ended up taking weeks to disappear—whoops.

That's my family. Sometimes wild and crazy. But always crazy beautiful. They make everything possible for me because they make me happy. I bring the fun and joy we have together into my music and everything else I do.

"I knew I was talented when I turned two. My dad [saw] it, my mom [saw] it, everybody saw that I was just talented. I've always wanted to be an entertainer."

CHAPTER 6
Talking to the Universe

In one on my favorite outfits, showing
Los Angeles some love!

Another thing that makes me strong and successful is having a spiritual practice. It's super important to me, and it's how I attract the right things into my life. My mom is a very spiritual person. She taught me all about manifesting and being in touch with the energetic universe that surrounds us.

You might be asking yourself, "What the heck is my girl Lay Lay talking about? What's manifesting?" Let me break it down for you a little bit. Manifesting is a practice where you focus on creating what you want in your life by imagining it, believing in it, and then making it happen. You can practice

manifesting to attract whatever you want—whether it's success in school, good health, or getting really good at something you love doing.

The secret behind manifestation is basically knowing that you get what you put out. Put out good vibes and say positive things, and you're most likely to get them back. Do the opposite and . . . oops. It probably won't go so good!

But manifesting only works if you talk to the energy of the universe and get close to what she wants for you. (I call the universe "she." She might be a "he" or a "they." I don't know. But to me, the universe is "she.")

Manifesting is sort of like when Luke, Yoda, or even Grogu (aka Baby Yoda) use the Force in *Star Wars*. They focus really hard on the energy around them so they can move mountains. When you're doing that, there's no limit to what you can do! You can live your wildest dreams. I'm proof.

At first, I didn't really believe in this type of stuff. But then I started trying it out. For example, if I said a negative thing, it would happen. Like if I said,

"No, I can't cook," then the next morning, I couldn't even pour my cereal straight into a bowl. And I was like, "Wait a minute. Did that just happen?"

So, I started thinking more positive things to see if

Finding peace in myself by working hard and staying positive.

they would happen, and they did! If I said out loud, "I don't know how to do it yet, but I know I can bake a cake," and then somehow, I'd figure out how to make a cake—and the frosting!

So I'm very into practicing manifestation now. Sometimes, when there's a full moon, I like to make a moon bath. I set all my crystals on the tub, and I talk to the universe and tell her what I want. I make a whole list of everything I want to achieve. And I take a candle and burn a list of all the negative things I don't want. (But please don't burn anything without a grown-up's help! It should only be done in a safe way!)

I make sure to say the right things every day now because the universe doesn't really care whether something is positive or if it's negative; she just brings you what you're asking for. And she only knows what you want if you tell her and set your intentions to make it happen.

Maybe that's where my superpower comes from. The universe knows how badly I want to perform perfectly when the cameras come on. She also knows I'm totally devoted to my career and put all my energy, love, and hard work into it, so she knows how to help me.

I think manifesting can help anyone who is dedicated to achieving big things in their life, but make sure you're not getting it twisted. Just because you practice manifestation and tell the universe what you want, that doesn't mean that she's going to drop everything you ask for right into your lap. She doesn't work alone. She needs to know you're with her.

I've learned that manifesting only works for me because I'm also willing to work hard to fulfill my dreams!

CHAPTER 7
Go Lay Lay Go!

Such a thrill to appear on the *Ellen* show!

Going viral and signing with Empire Records were just the first steps of my career. About a month after I signed my record deal, I took my talents to daytime TV.

In September 2018, I was invited to appear on *The Ellen DeGeneres Show*. It was an incredible opportunity to perform, not just before a live studio audience, but to over two million people who were watching the show every day from home.

I didn't tell anybody, but while I was excited to be on the show, I was also a little bit—okay, maybe a lot—nervous. Two million people is a lot of people. I got famous rapping to one person in a car!

Before the show, I kept practicing

the freestyle that I was planning to perform because it was an old freestyle and I hadn't done it in a while. My dad was like, "Okay, Lay Lay, you got it?" And I was like, "Yeah, yeah, yeah. Don't worry—I'm good. I'm good."

But when I got to the studio for rehearsal, I messed up every single time I tried to do it! Remember when I kept missing all those shots at the Rockets game? It was like that—but worse. I'm not actually a basketball player, so if I had missed that shot it wouldn't have been that big a deal. It's not like I'd be missing out on a career in the WNBA!

But I *am* a professional rapper. And a rapper who can't rap during the biggest moment of her career won't keep getting props from people like 50 Cent. I broke down right before our final rehearsal. I cried, "Oh my God. I can't believe that I practiced twenty times in a row and still keep messing up! What is going on?" I realized I had one last chance before the show to get it right and get my swagger back. But then, that last time, I messed up, too! Ellen was worried. So was I!

A big audience of people poured into the studio. Ellen called me out in front of the cameras and then . . . OMG, thank the universe! *Super* Lay Lay showed up. I killed it! It was one of my best performances. I think Ellen was surprised, too! But I was a big success on the show, and the clip went viral.

Around this time, I also got to meet singer Neyo in the halls of *Rolling Out* magazine.

👑 👑 👑

Another fun TV appearance I did was on the MTV show *Wild 'N Out*, hosted by Nick Cannon. On *Wild 'N Out*, two teams of rappers—the Red Squad and the Black Squad—roast each other in comedy games that are really funny. The show ends with a segment called Wildstyle, where a rapper from one team goes up against a rapper from the other team. You have to be ready to do a real, off-the-dome freestyle because you don't know what the other rapper is going to say to you.

I was the only kid going up against some grown-up rappers who do Wildstylin' for a living. Not to mention, I actually didn't know I was going on the show until the day of the taping. My dad said to me that morning, "Guess what? You have the chance to go on *Wild 'N Out*!" And I was like, "I'm just finding out now?!" I really wanted to do it; I just would've liked a little more heads-up!

When it came to Wildstyle, I was worried. I told the people on set: "I'm afraid to do it. Because if I mess up, I'm going to be really upset with myself."

But of course, I changed my mind and went on

anyway. I got out there, and DC Young Fly, one of the regular cast members, really tried to put me down. He made fun of me for being a kid who doesn't pay her own bills. When I listened to him, I was thinking, *Oh no! I'm on national TV and you're*

roasting me like this? Talking to me like I'm a snot-nosed kid with no lunch money? I was like, "Are you really trying me right now?" I got really mad and the words just started flowing:

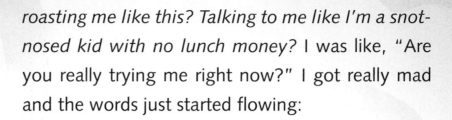

All right, okay, let's do it
All y'all wack like your outfit
I've been making money
since six
I work for me, y'all work
for Nick!

It brought down the house, and Nick Cannon immediately declared my team the winner!

That was a true freestyle: no preparation and no rehearsal. I just channeled my inner rapper—and won for the Black Squad!

My performances on *Ellen* and *Wild 'N Out* were so important to my development as an artist. Doing well on *Ellen* showed everyone who was watching that I wasn't just some kid who got lucky

I was the only kid on *Wild 'N Out*, but that didn't stop me from winning the battle for my team. My championship belt was almost as big as me!

I appeared in my first Macy's Thanksgiving
Day Parade in 2019.

on Instagram. And *Wild 'N Out* gave me a chance to battle, which has been a big part of hip-hop culture since before rap music was even popular. Both appearances helped me prove that I was a real rapper who could step in front of big audiences with big names and not just move the crowd . . . but totally kill it!

"The advice that I have is to always keep going. If you have something that you really wanna do, then just do it."

CHAPTER 8

The Fresh Born Unicorn Meets Dapper Dan

I like to have fun with my style, and I love my drip. "Drip" is like "swagger" or "cool," but only in terms of your appearance.

If you've looked at my social media, you know my drip is influenced by logos from big fashion houses. I love Gucci, Balenciaga, and Louis Vuitton. I even used to have a multicolored LV logo painted on my bedroom wall! Can you blame me? It reminded me that I'm living my dreams and helped to keep me grateful for what I've achieved.

So it was natural that my love for tricked-out logo designs would lead me to a designer known as Dapper Dan. When I first saw what he was doing in fashion, I thought, *This look is so me!* I'd seen his specially made outfits for Beyoncé, Lizzo, and Billie Eilish, to name a few. Those looks really *dripped*.

I wanted to learn more about Dapper Dan, and what I discovered was incredible! It took my mind on an adventure into the history of fashion and my favorite music.

See, back in the early days of hip-hop, Dapper Dan made clothes that rappers would wear when they wanted to flex and make everyone else jealous. Dapper Dan had a shop in Harlem, the historically Black neighborhood in New York where a lot of famous artists and musicians come from. In the 1980s, Dapper Dan became a legend by sewing together different fabrics to create incredible, high-end streetwear in ways nobody ever had before! If you look up album covers or music videos from the 1980s and 1990s, you'll see legends like Salt-N-Pepa and LL Cool J wearing amazing Dapper Dan outfits. Because he broke the rules by taking garments from big fashion houses and remaking them with hip-hop swagger, rappers called him a fashion outlaw!

But being an outlaw got him into trouble when the big fashion brands realized he was using their logos and fabrics. They didn't understand streetwear, and they put him out of business. And for years, nobody knew what happened to him. But the legend of Dapper Dan grew.

Then, in 2017, a Gucci model appeared at a big fashion show in a jacket that looked just like one Dapper Dan had designed in the 1980s. People called the company out on social media and said, "Hey, how come you're hijacking Dapper Dan's style and not giving him credit?"

Gucci's famous designer didn't deny it. He let people know Dapper Dan was one of his biggest influences. And a lot of the other biggest designers in the world said the same thing.

That's all it took for Dapper Dan to come back in a BIG way! He signed a deal with Gucci, opened up his own spot in Harlem in a beautiful brownstone, and was right back on top.

So I knew Dapper Dan was the GOAT. I'd seen pictures of Dapper Dan's styles on classic hip-hop rappers and some of the biggest pop stars today. I'd seen Salma Hayek wearing Dapper Dan at the Oscars! But I hadn't seen a kid in Dapper Dan—yet. I thought to myself, *I need to be the first one!* So, I sent him a DM on Instagram. And I was so excited when Dapper Dan invited me to visit him!

When I arrived at his "atelier" in Harlem (that's what he calls his studio), Dapper Dan walked outside to greet me. So many people stopped to say hi to him and show respect. He was wearing the sharpest suit I've ever seen, but at the same time, he was so down to earth. It seemed like everybody in Harlem worshipped him!

Here I am in Harlem for my fitting with
fashion icon Dapper Dan!

You don't just get a Dapper Dan 'fit at the mall: He makes something unique for you, and he'll never make the same thing for anybody else. He made me a pair of customized Gucci logo pink overalls with flowered suspenders and the Dapper Dan patch on the back. It's so dope!

Years from now, I'll be able to say, "I have a Dapper Dan piece," and I made history as the first

Still looking fresh with Sugar and Sweets from Tha Slay Gang.

kid to have a Dapper Dan outfit styled for me!

Dapper Dan told me we're friends. And that means the most to me! Having the chance to be friends with a legend is even more important than getting to wear his clothes. And getting to spend time with him made me feel like part of hip-hop history in a way that I'll never forget.

CHAPTER 9

Work Hard,
Play Harder

You can't school people if you're afraid to get schooled. This is me showing off some of my early merch. I can't believe that now I'm putting out an official product line with Nickelodeon!

I may be an entertainer who likes her style, but I learned early on that life isn't just about how you look. What's even more important is how you think. A good education is key to understanding the world and learning how to do things for yourself. So, I'm not just about songs and clothes. I'm also about the books!

I work hard on my schoolwork just like I do on my music. Okay, not *too* hard! It's not like homework is my favorite thing in the world. But I do it and I'm committed to getting smarter every day.

I used to go to a private school, but that became too much for me when I had to be up all night in the studio recording new tracks and then get up early the next morning to go to school. It just didn't work. There was no way I was going to be able to do my best at school *and* in the studio without a special game plan.

So, I started homeschooling instead. I felt most comfortable with an online program that I can do on my own time. I do classes every day, and I work for one hour on each subject until I've accomplished that day's goals.

Online schools like mine are a great option for performers, student athletes, and kids from military

I'm always ready to learn!

families who aren't in one place all the time. It also has really good options for kids dealing with bullying and kids with chronic illnesses or other special needs. I really appreciate that it lets me follow my dreams and still get an education.

Homeschooling is good for me now, but I'd love to go to a real high school. I might be touring the world by then, but for my senior year, I'd really like to go in person! I don't want to grow up and feel like I missed out completely on all those high school experiences. Plus, all my friends will be there!

My dad says I won't be able to go to school without security. I think he's afraid the other students won't act right. I know he's just looking out for me. Still, I'd feel good if I could go in that last year. Fingers crossed!

If you're working hard on your schoolwork (and a career!), it's also super important to have hobbies that let you cut loose and just have fun. You definitely don't need to be a celebrity to know that doing simple things for yourself is good for your soul.

So what are my jams when it comes to small pleasures? I like to Hula-Hoop. I like to jump rope. I like go-karting. I like going to Urban Air to jump on the trampolines. I still love skating a lot; it's just a little harder to get to the rink because of the crowds that find me.

And I love to have a good time during the holidays, too. Holidays make the whole year special!

Halloween is my favorite. But you want to know something funny about me? I love Halloween, but I'm very scared of it—even though I know being scared is supposed to be part of the fun. I love the candy, but when it comes to scary costumes and all that extra stuff, no way, not for me! I don't like haunted houses. I don't even like trick-or-treating because I'm afraid someone is going to jump out of a bush and scare me! During Halloween, I usually eat a lot of candy, stay home, and watch scary movies.

Okay, I guess I like scary stuff when it's on a television screen—just not in my neighborhood!

"I focus on my school and I focus on my career."

CHAPTER 10
Move Like I Move

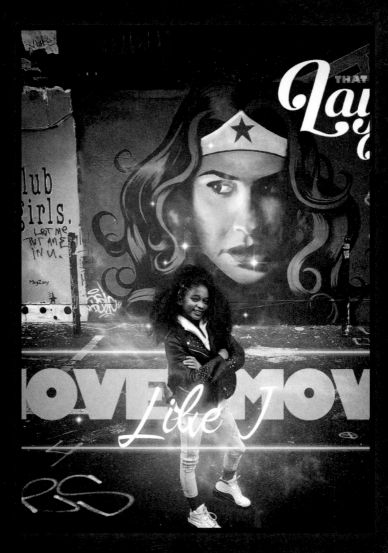

The way I dance and move is a big part of who I am as a performer!

*I*f you're going to be a great performer—I want to be Great with a capital *G*!—you've got to bring it in more ways than one. And that means practicing multiple talents.

When it comes to hip-hop, not every great rapper is a great dancer. Some people just bring a

My first song ever was "Move Like I Move," which I did with my dad.

ton of energy to the stage. But I want to be huge like Beyoncé, so that means I have to show moves you can't take your eyes off!

I've always loved to dance! Since I was little, it's always been my thing. I paid close attention to people who could dance, how they moved, and their choreography. I started training almost as soon as I could walk!

Like with my flow, I put a lot of time into perfecting my moves. When I was five, I started training with my first teacher, and I studied with her until I was eleven. When you see me do some killer moves in my video "Stop Playin," it's not just natural talent or luck. It's me hitting my marks because I'll do take after take until the performance is right for the camera.

If you want to be good at something, you've got to practice, let yourself fall, and get it wrong a thousand times until you finally figure it out. Then you can start having more fun with it and throw your own style on top of it!

But you can never stop studying because there's

always something else to learn. Like a tree, you have to branch out. Really amazing artists have a way of bringing in new influences to what they do to make their performances stand apart from others. Or they try something that doesn't come so naturally to continue growing and keep them on their toes.

Lately, I've been trying to do this by taking ballet! It is *literally* keeping me on my toes! I really like it, but it's definitely not easy. I'm used to hip-hop dancing, which is fast and spontaneous. So ballet is teaching me patience because it is disciplined and *slllloooowwwwww*.

When I first started, I hated the strictness of ballet. I was like, "Where's the *umph*? Like, what is this?"

My godmother, Sarah, said to me not too long ago, "I used to try to teach you ballet, and you would just be running around

Ballet moves more slowly than hip-hop . . .

everywhere. You refused to pay attention."

I said, "Yeah, probably because I was three!" I don't think I was really focusing on my pliés at the time.

I had to grow into loving it. But I'm glad I did because ballet teaches me to breathe, to focus, and to have patience. I admit, I'm still really trying to work on the patience part. But ballet also teaches balance, so now whatever dance styles I'm doing, at least I'm less likely to fall on my face!

I also started taking yoga. I like yoga—but it's also really slow and takes concentration! Like I said, I'm just a fast person. I like to move! But sometimes you just need to slow down and be calm.

If you think about it, a person is sort of like a song. You can't go along at one fast speed the whole time or you get boring. It's good when a song starts fast, then slows down at the bridge or brings in a different tempo. So, I like what I've learned with ballet and yoga because by slowing me down, it expands my options on how to approach dance—and life! We all need to explore multiple sides of ourselves.

That's something I've learned by slowing down. As much as I have to work on the things I'm good at to *stay* good at them, it's just as important that I work on things I'm not good at. That way I strengthen different parts of myself and stay interesting—as a performer and as a person!

. . . but it keeps me on my toes!

CHAPTER 11

On Tour with Tha Slay Gang

I 🖤 New York!

I put so much time into dancing and rehearsal because when I go out on tour and perform my music live, I really want to slay! My goal is to give the audience a show that they'll love and that I'll be proud of.

Touring is where a performer always has to prove herself. No matter how many people are watching, it's never easy. At my first shows, I might have seen *only* twenty people in the audience. When the crowd is so small, you see *every* face. That was strange at first, being so close to the audience. But I realized

that everyone at those shows was a true fan. They didn't come out because I was popular. They came because they loved what I was doing before other people had caught on. That made for something special in each performance.

I remember one show where there was a baby who knew all my song lyrics and did not stop dancing. Between songs, I called out, "How old are you?" and her mom answered, "She's one!" Maybe one day I'll write a rhyme about that fan who as a "bay-bay loved her some Lay Lay."

Although there were great times like this, the small crowds could get me down. I wanted bigger audiences, but they didn't come right away. Sometimes I felt bad and sad enough that I wanted to quit. Instead, I decided to tell the universe, "I don't want just twenty people at my shows." I asked her for more, and I decided I wouldn't quit until she gave them to me.

Things changed fast. Three or four months later, I was getting 5,000 people at every single show. And I was like, "Wow! Look at how far I've come!" Then I told the universe I wanted *more* people at my shows, and she was like, "Okay, I got you. I got you."

Before I knew it, I was getting 20,000 people at a show. It's like she knew I could handle it. It's funny, but I'm a lot more comfortable and relaxed playing to 20,000 people than to 20. Maybe because when there's a big audience, I can't really see single

faces staring at me. I'm just seeing everybody's heads bobbing to the music. I feel all those people's emotions moving along with me. And I can work with that!

For me, it's who I perform with that makes what I do extra special. Touring wouldn't be touring if I wasn't out there with my girls. Four of my closest friends have toured with me a lot. Lanaya Cooper, who's known as Sweets, and Mylie Stone, who we call Sugar, are my Slay Gang now. But I started with Tatiana Romero and Ariana Baez. You need your

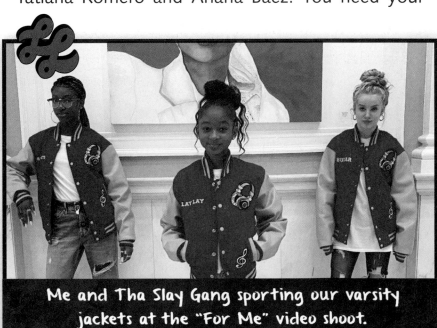

Me and Tha Slay Gang sporting our varsity jackets at the "For Me" video shoot.

girls around to keep it fun when you're spending hours on a bus trip from Dayton, Ohio, to Long Island City, New York.

But a tour isn't only about being onstage. A lot happens between shows that makes being on the road something you can never forget. Like the time I was in a tour bus with Sugar and Sweets and some of our road crew. There was a second bus with some other young talent on the tour. What we didn't know was that they had water guns on the other bus. Not small ones, either. The big Super Soaker kind!

When we stopped for food, they snuck up and ambushed us as a prank. They sprayed us with so much water that we were sopping wet. So, as we were riding along, we came up with a plan. At our next stop, my assistant snuck the water guns out of their bus when they weren't looking. Then, when they came back near their bus, we just went crazy spraying water at them.

But we didn't actually get *all* their water weapons. They were carrying around a few. It became an all-out water war! This was only an hour before our

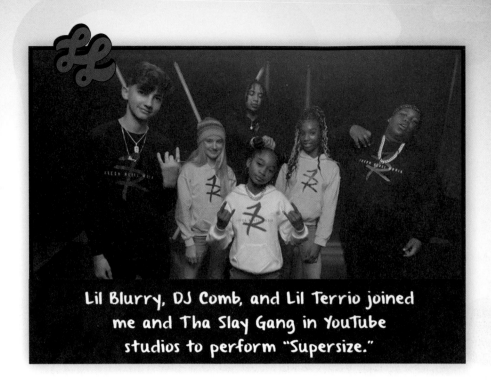

Lil Blurry, DJ Comb, and Lil Terrio joined
me and Tha Slay Gang in YouTube
studios to perform "Supersize."

show. When we finally ran out of water, there wasn't a dry person in the whole crew. Oh, and did I forget to mention, we were in our stage clothes the whole time?

We got to the show just before it started, so we didn't have time to change or fix ourselves. We were just hoping our hair wasn't too wild and the audience wouldn't notice how wet we were. But when we got offstage and looked at ourselves in the dressing room mirrors, we realized we were total train wrecks—actually, more like shipwrecks!

I thought, *This is how we looked? This is how we went onstage? Really?!* I couldn't believe it!

Tours are like that. They're a lot of work—but they're also a lot of fun. I can't wait to see what happens on my next one!

Me and Tha Slay Gang have a lot of good times. But we have our ups and downs, too. No matter how famous or successful you get, everyone has friendship troubles sometimes. When you start blowing up, you have more and more responsibility. Your career can take you away from people you love, which changes your relationships.

I'm off in different places a lot, whereas Sugar and Sweets always live in Atlanta when we're not on tour. No matter whether I'm in New York, LA, or Kentucky, I do my best to keep in touch with my girls every day. But it's not the same as being there with them. So, they've become really close with each other because they get to spend more time together.

That means I'm a little bit on the outside

sometimes. I wish it wasn't the case. But I've got to be understanding and give my BFFs a chance to adjust to me being away so often—and be kind to myself so I don't get too sad about it. Because I know that at the end of the day, those are my girls. We always have a good time when we can get together!

As we grow up, we're learning to be kinder to each other. When we were younger, we'd argue about *a lot* of stupid stuff. On the bus someone might complain, "Why are you chewing so loud?" And we would end up arguing about how loud one

Slayin' at the video shoot for "Long Hair."

It's not just about the music. It's also about who you make it with.

of us was eating a bag of chips. Now when we talk about those times, we realize how we argued about the silliest things! I'm just so lucky that I have super talented best friends who never make me go on the road alone. They're always ready to get back out there with me.

"As soon as I touch that mic, I'm ready to turn up onstage. There's no going back."

CHAPTER 12

Gotta Eat Right

I nearly froze trying to be cute for the Macy's Parade in 2019. I didn't wear gloves, socks, or winter shoes! Next time I'll keep it fresh while taking better care of myself.

*I*f you're going to tour a lot of cities to perform and make appearances, you gotta eat right. If you're not taking care of yourself, you won't have the energy to show up every night, remember your rhymes, and hit your steps. I definitely take care of both my mental and physical health because otherwise I know I'd burn out fast!

My dad taught me that important lesson because he knows I'm the kind of person who would try to push through anything—even when I needed rest or was feeling sick—just to get the job done. My dad always reminds me that I really have to put myself first so that I don't end up in bed sick from overdoing it!

"You have to make sure you're eating right," he used to tell me, "because you work a lot and then you forget about eating. You can't just eat once a day."

I admit, I don't like to eat breakfast. Even though it's supposed to be the most important meal of the day, I'm just not a breakfast person. So, my mom and my dad are always on me about that type of stuff!

I'm a pescatarian, which means that the only meat I eat is fish. I have a sensitive stomach, so fish is the best thing for my system and it gives me the nutrition I need. But it's funny that I became pescatarian because I don't actually like fish that much! I don't like sushi, and I'm also never going for the all-you-can-eat specials at Red Lobster. I only like salmon, and I hardly like that. I just eat it because it's the best source of protein and iron for me.

Thankfully, I am a kid who loves her fruits and vegetables. And not just eating them. I like to grow them, too! There's a garden in our yard where I grow kale and banana peppers. It should also have strawberries, but the squirrels keep eating them. They don't steal my blueberries and blackberries for some reason, though, which is good because those are my favorite fruits.

I'm also growing tomatoes, spinach, onions,

lemongrass, and lavender—the last two smell so good! If the entertainment business ever gets slow for me, maybe I can have a second career as a farmer. They'll call me "That Girl Hay Hay!"

But please don't go thinking I'm a perfect eater. I do love some foods that aren't exactly healthy.

When I was little, my parents would ask me, "What do you want to eat?"

I'd always answer, "Macaroni!"

"Well, what do you want on the side?"

"French fries."

OMG, I love fries! And I still eat that. I get macaroni and cheese with french fries whenever I can. It's a weird pair. But honestly, it's everything that I want in a meal!

And I love Italian food. I would eat pizza and pasta every day if I could. Any type of pasta, to be honest. I like Cajun pasta, spaghetti Alfredo, and even the green pesto sauce! I love pasta especially because it keeps me going when I'm on tour and gives me the energy I need to put on amazing shows for my fans!

CHAPTER 13
Tha Lil Big Dripper!

Making music I love has made me part
of an Empire!

People often ask me, "Lay Lay, what is it like to be the youngest female rap artist ever signed to a major label?" It always seems weird to think of myself that way.

When I signed to my label, Empire Records, I didn't know I made history. Then I googled "youngest female rapper," and *I* popped up. I was like, "Wait a minute! That can't be right . . ." I had to look it up again because I didn't believe it!

I know it's something I've accomplished only because I've been dedicated to my music for as long as I can remember. I'm constantly inspired to be creative, but I've had to sacrifice a lot of normal growing up for it.

Most of my inspiration for my songs comes from everyday things I'm doing or that are going on in the real world, whether it's hanging with my friends, go-karting, or dancing. If I'm having a bad day, or if I'm sad, mad, or happy, writing lyrics is a great

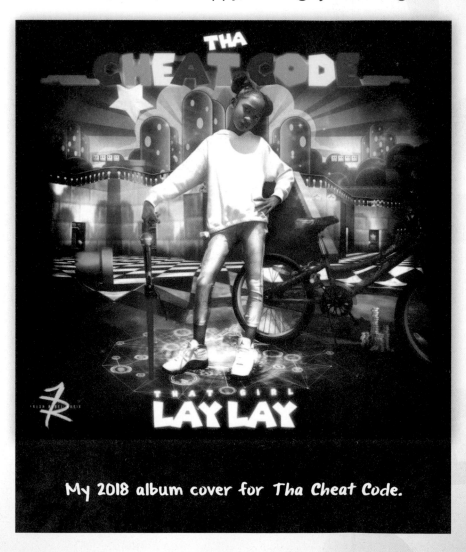

My 2018 album cover for *Tha Cheat Code*.

outlet for me. Whatever I'm feeling is my material. What comes out really just depends on the time, the place, or even the season.

I'm not someone who wants to break her arm

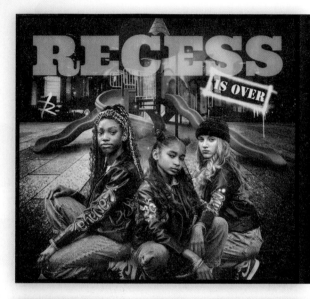

With Tha Slay Gang on the cover of our 2020 album, Recess Is Over.

The photo for my Lil Big Dripper album was shot in Puerto Rico.

patting herself on the back, but I'm really proud of the music I've made as an artist on Empire Records. I have one song with Young Dolph, called "Breezy." That's one of my favorite songs to this day—it's

I love the song "Breezy" that I did with Young Dolph!

Me on the go in this sample cover of my "Go Lay Lay Go" single!

incredible! I made it knowing it was a track kids would love!

But even though I'm still feeling the music I've already recorded, I'm always looking forward to the next thing. And I'm always ready for whatever comes next because I'm all about that preparation and practice.

A lot of people will say, "Oh, Lay Lay, I want to be a rapper like you."

I tell them, "It's not just rapping—being a performing artist takes so much more than you might think."

In their eyes, I'm just having fun. I *do* have fun, but I'm also awake and working in a sound studio at 4:00 a.m. The entertainment business isn't just glitz and glam. I always tell the people who think I'm living an around-the-clock party: "Don't just pursue a career as a performer because you think it's something really fun. It comes with a lot of discipline and dedication."

Most people really just want what fame looks like. And I get it. I'm not *that* different. I watch

Beyoncé and see all the famous rappers. It used to be easy for me, too, to say, "Yeah, that's what I want," not fully realizing all that comes with being famous. Some people realize it too late, or they don't have good guidance or take care of themselves and get lost in the fame game.

Entertainers—including rappers—tend to have entourages with them all the time. Sure, they have their assistants and managers they need around, but there also might be people they started out with who aren't healthy for them anymore or people who don't need to be there 24/7. Those people usually just want to get something for nothing.

If you've got the wrong people and the wrong energy around you, it's going to mess with your mind and your heart. You might think everybody loves you and is your friend, but then if they take advantage of you or bring bad energy to your life, it can do more harm than good. Music has had way too many talented people get hurt by having the wrong people in their entourage.

That's why I'm so grateful I have a dad who

knows the business, a mom who helps me keep my spirit right, and enough kid wisdom to be around people with the right energy. If the energy's not right, I don't want it in my life!

That's how I am and that's how I'm going to stay. I want to be successful and feel good about my life. And guess what? You can be the same way.

Make sure you spend time with people who give good energy to you. If someone makes you feel bad whenever you're around them or wants you to do things you know aren't right for you, it's okay to say, "No, thank you. Get to steppin'!"

"I have to speak about what I say, what is real."

CHAPTER 14
All the Way Lit

Representing at the BET Hip-Hop Awards in 2018.

*B*ecause I love hip-hop so much, you might think that succeeding in rap was my only dream.

But it wasn't. My even bigger dream was to have my own TV show! A lot of Hollywood movie stars, like Queen Latifah, Will Smith, and Ice Cube, started off as rappers. And I'm doing my best to follow in their footsteps.

In the spring of 2021, I moved to Los Angeles with my family to start filming my show *That Girl Lay Lay* for Nickelodeon. Can you believe it? I told the universe I wanted to have a TV show. I believed in what I wanted with every bone in my body. Then it happened! The universe really does help make everything happen for me. She's like my fairy godmother.

When I was little, I told my dad, "I need to be in LA. That's my town!" I have a birthmark on my neck that everybody mistakes for a tattoo. And, no

In my happy place at the Nickelodeon Studios in Los Angeles.

kidding, it is actually in the shape of the city of Los Angeles. It's like I was born with a map on my neck so the raps coming out of my mouth would know what direction to take me. And I'm so happy that now I actually get to live and work there.

That Girl Lay Lay is produced by the incredible Will Packer, who's made super-funny movies like *Girls Trip*. I play an avatar from a personal affirmation app that magically comes to life. The show is about my character and her best friend, Sadie, who's a

Walking with the stars on the Hollywood Walk of Fame!

real teenager, as we go through life in high school while discovering who we truly are as friends and individuals. I love that my character is very funny and comes to life from an app that gives out positive thoughts—that's so me!

My show is filled with a lot of humor, which is perfect because I love comedy. Mindy Kaling is one of my inspirations and so is Tiffany Haddish. I hope I'm half as good as them at making people laugh because if I am, then I'll be slayin'.

I really admire dramatic actresses, too! Some of my favorites are Angela Bassett and Regina King. They broke through at an Oscar level for their incredible work on-screen. They're killing it out there! It wasn't that long ago that very few Black actresses were getting leading roles. I'm inspired by their legacy! And I'm trying to be an inspiration to young Black girls who get to see somebody my age starring on TV. For such a long time, we didn't get chances like this. I want them to know they can do it, too!

I'll never forget the day I got my first script. My dad sent it to me late at night when he thought I'd be asleep. I knew it was coming, so I woke up at midnight and checked my email. I opened it, and right there on the title page of the script it read, *That Girl Lay Lay*.

I jumped for joy!

I ran around the whole house waking everybody up. When one of your dreams come true, sometimes you have to wake people up from theirs to share it!

CHAPTER 15

That's a Rap

That's my story so far. I'm only a teenager, so I know I've got a lot more life to live and plenty of things to learn. I'm still discovering new things every day.

I'm just so happy to be on the right path for me. Everything I'm doing really fits my personality. I know who I am, what I want to do, and how I want to do it. So I don't ever listen to anyone who says I can't!

There were people who told me I was too young to have a recording contract. Others said I was too young to be on TV. I don't listen to them. Age is nothing but a number. I do what I love—what I *really* love. I've learned that if I

work hard at my goals and believe in them like my life depends on it, I can accomplish anything!

But I've also learned that doing something well enough to make you famous means there are pressures you can't hide from. That's when having positive people in my life who support me makes all the difference.

Some people want fame and celebrity without being prepared for it. I always want to be prepared! I want to stay positive, always do what I love, slay all day, keep drippin', and never stop being a fresh born unicorn!

And I'm ready for whatever the universe throws at me next.